Brothers

By Shirleyann Costigan
Illustrated by Yoriko Ito

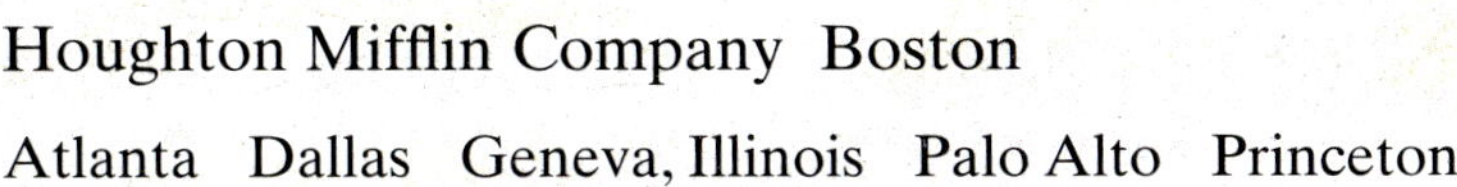

Houghton Mifflin Company Boston
Atlanta Dallas Geneva, Illinois Palo Alto Princeton

When my brother comes home
for a visit, we have fun together.

We play basketball in our driveway.
“Catch!” he calls.
Sometimes I don’t catch the ball.

But sometimes I do.

We swim in the pool down the street.
“Come on!” he says. “Jump!”
Sometimes I don’t jump in.

But sometimes I do.

We watch monster movies.
"Now you can look," he says.
Sometimes I don't open my eyes.

But sometimes I do.

We skate in the park.
"You can do it!" he says.
Sometimes I don't let go.

But sometimes I do.

We ride the roller coaster.
"Want to go again?" he asks.
Sometimes I don't want to ride again.

But sometimes I do.

The days go by so fast
when my brother visits.
Then it's time for him to go.

We drive to the bus station.
We have fun together right up
to the end!

But then the visit is really over.
"Come back soon," I say.

"I will," he says.
"I always do!"
And he always does.